Whys for a Successful Mindset: Uncovering the Whys That Drive a Winning Mindset

"The Essential Role of Self-Reflection and Curiosity in Reaching Your Full Potential"

© **Max Fortune**

The author would like to thank all the people who have contributed to the creation of this book, including family, friends, and colleagues. Special thanks go to [names of individuals who made significant contributions].

Table of Contents

Chapter 1
Introduction

Have you ever felt like you're just going through the motions in life, without any real sense of purpose or direction? Do you find yourself stuck in a rut, unsure of how to break free and achieve your goals? If so, you're not alone. Many people struggle with finding their path to success, and it's not always easy to know where to start.

However, there is a powerful tool that can help you gain clarity and direction on the road to success: asking yourself "why." By asking yourself reflective questions and digging deep to uncover your motivations and desires, you can create a clear roadmap for achieving your goals and living a fulfilling life.

The "why" behind our goals is often more important than the goal itself. When we have a deep understanding of why we want something, we are more likely to stay committed and motivated, even when things get tough. By contrast, if we don't have a clear understanding of our why, we may lose steam and give up when faced with challenges or setbacks.

The road to success is paved with whys. When we take the time to ask ourselves why we want something, we are able to uncover the deeper motivations and desires that drive us forward. We can gain a clearer sense of our strengths and weaknesses, our core values and beliefs, and our short-term and long-term goals.

In this guide to self-discovery and achievement, we will explore the power of asking "why" and how it can help you achieve your goals and live a fulfilling life. We will delve into the types of questions you can ask yourself to gain clarity and direction, and we'll provide practical tips and tools for using the power of "why" to unlock your full potential.

One important thing to keep in mind is that asking yourself "why" can be a challenging and sometimes uncomfortable process. It requires self-reflection and honesty with oneself, which can be difficult for some people. However, the benefits of uncovering your motivations and desires are well worth the effort.

By asking yourself why you want something, you can get to the root of your motivations and identify what truly matters to you. This can help you create a sense of purpose and direction in your life, and make it easier to set and achieve meaningful goals. Additionally, when you have a clear understanding of your why, it becomes easier to communicate your goals and desires to others, which can help you build stronger relationships and gain support from those around you.

Another important aspect of asking why is that it allows you to evaluate your goals and make sure they are aligned with your values and beliefs. Sometimes we set goals based on external pressures or societal expectations, rather than our own desires. By asking yourself why you want something, you can determine if it truly aligns with your values and if it's worth pursuing.

Finally, asking why can help you overcome obstacles and challenges on the road to success. When you have a clear understanding of your motivations and desires, you can tap into a sense of resilience and determination that can help you persevere through difficult times. You can also identify potential roadblocks and develop strategies for overcoming them, which can help you stay on track and achieve your goals.

In conclusion, the road to success is indeed paved with whys. By asking yourself reflective questions and digging deep to uncover your motivations and desires, you can gain clarity and direction on your path to achievement. So take the time to ask yourself why, and discover the power of self-discovery and achievement. So if you're ready to start on the road to success, join us on this journey of self-discovery and achievement. Together, we'll pave the way to a brighter future, one "why" at a time.

Chapter 2
Getting to Know Yourself: Uncovering Your Core Values and Beliefs

At the heart of self-discovery is the process of getting to know yourself. Understanding your core values and beliefs is essential in finding your path to success, as they shape your thoughts, actions, and decisions. Identifying and aligning with your values and beliefs can help you develop a sense of purpose and direction, and create a strong foundation for achieving your goals.

So how can you uncover your core values and beliefs? It starts with self-reflection. Take the time to think about what matters most to you, what drives you, and what you stand for. Consider your past experiences, both positive and negative, and what you learned from them. Reflect on your strengths and weaknesses, your passions and interests, and your relationships with others. Think about what makes you happy, fulfilled, and satisfied.

As you reflect, you may find it helpful to write down your thoughts and insights. Keeping a journal or using a note-taking app can be a great way to capture your ideas and track your progress over time. You may also find it helpful to talk with trusted friends, family members, or mentors who can offer insights and perspectives on your values and beliefs.

Once you have a sense of what matters most to you, you can begin to identify your core values and beliefs. Values are the guiding principles that shape your behavior and actions, such as honesty, integrity, and compassion. Beliefs are the ideas and attitudes that you hold to be true, such as your religious or political views, or your beliefs about the nature of the world and your place in it.

To identify your core values and beliefs, consider the following questions:

- What do I stand for?
- What are my guiding principles?
- What do I believe in?
- What are my priorities?
- What makes me feel fulfilled and satisfied?

As you answer these questions, look for common themes and patterns in your responses. These can help you identify your core values and beliefs and gain a deeper understanding of yourself.

Once you have identified your core values and beliefs, it's important to align your actions and decisions with them. This can help you stay true to yourself and make choices that are in line with your values and beliefs. It can also help you build trust and credibility with others, as they see that you are consistent and authentic in your behavior.

As you identify your core values and beliefs, it's important to remember that they may evolve and change over time. What was important to you in the past may not be as important now, and new experiences and insights may lead you to reevaluate your beliefs and values. It's important to stay open to these changes and continue to reflect on what matters most to you.

Once you have a clear understanding of your core values and beliefs, you can use them as a guide in making important decisions and setting goals. For example, if one of your core values is creativity, you may want to explore career paths or hobbies that allow you to express your creativity. If one of your core beliefs is the importance of community, you may want to seek out volunteer opportunities or join a social group that aligns with this value.

Aligning your actions and decisions with your core values and beliefs can also help you build stronger relationships with others. When you are authentic and true to yourself, others can sense this and are more likely to trust and respect you. This can help you build a network of supportive relationships that can help you achieve your goals and navigate the challenges of life.

Uncovering your core values and beliefs is an essential step in the process of self-discovery. By reflecting on what matters most to you and identifying your guiding principles, you can create a strong foundation for achieving your goals and living a fulfilling life. So take the time to get to know yourself, and embrace the power of your core values and beliefs.

It's also important to recognize that identifying your core values and beliefs is an ongoing process. As you continue to grow and learn, you may discover new aspects of yourself and your values and beliefs may shift. So don't be afraid to revisit this process regularly and continue to reflect on what matters most to you.

Uncovering your core values and beliefs is to identify any conflicts or contradictions that may exist. For example, you may value creativity and innovation, but also hold beliefs about the importance of stability and security. These values may come into conflict when making decisions about career or lifestyle choices. By recognizing these conflicts, you can work to resolve them and find a balance that aligns with your core values and beliefs.

One should note that his core values and beliefs may be influenced by external factors such as culture, family, or societal norms. While it's important to stay true to yourself, it's also important to consider the perspectives and values of others and how they may impact your own values and beliefs. This can help you develop empathy and understanding for those with different perspectives and make more informed decisions that are in line with your own values and beliefs.

Another important aspect of uncovering your core values and beliefs is to take action based on them. This means setting goals and making decisions that align with your values and beliefs, even when it may be challenging or require stepping outside of your comfort zone. This can help you build confidence and resilience, as well as a sense of fulfillment and purpose in your life.

Uncovering your core values and beliefs is not a one-time event, but an ongoing process. As you experience new things and gain new insights, your values and beliefs may shift and evolve. By staying open to these changes and continuing to reflect on what matters most to you, you can create a strong foundation for personal growth and achievement.

Another important aspect of identifying your core values and beliefs is to understand how they may impact your relationships with others. Your values and beliefs may be different from those around you, and this can create challenges in personal and professional relationships. However, by communicating your values and beliefs with honesty and openness, you can create stronger connections with others who share similar values and beliefs, and find common ground with those who may have different perspectives.

It's also important to know that identifying your core values and beliefs is not just about achieving personal success, but about making a positive impact on the world around you. By living your values and beliefs with intention and purpose, you can contribute to a better future for yourself and others. This may involve taking action on issues that align with your values, supporting causes that are important to you, or using your talents and skills to make a difference in your community or the world at large.

Uncovering your core values and beliefs is a deeply personal process that may involve facing difficult truths about yourself and your life. It's important to approach this process with compassion and self-care, and to seek support from trusted friends, family members, or professionals if needed. By embracing this process with curiosity and openness, you can unlock a deeper understanding of yourself and your potential for success and fulfillment.

The process of identifying your core values and beliefs can be challenging and may require deep introspection. It's not uncommon for individuals to have conflicting values or beliefs that can be difficult to reconcile. In these cases, it's important to stay curious and non-judgmental towards yourself, and to approach the process with an open mind and heart.

One way to begin identifying your core values and beliefs is to start by reflecting on your life experiences and what has been most meaningful and fulfilling to you. Consider the times when you felt most alive, engaged, and in flow. What activities or experiences were you engaged in? What values or beliefs were being expressed during those moments? Taking note of these experiences and the associated values and beliefs can provide valuable insight into what matters most to you.

Another useful exercise is to consider what values or beliefs you would want to pass on to future generations. Imagine that you are passing on a legacy to your children, grandchildren, or other loved ones. What values or beliefs would you want them to embody? This can help to uncover what is most important to you and what you want to be remembered for.

Your core values and beliefs may change over time, and that this is a natural part of personal growth and development. As you experience new things and gain new insights, your values and beliefs may shift and evolve. By staying open to these changes and continuing to reflect on what matters most to you, you can create a strong foundation for personal growth and achievement.

One key benefit of identifying your core values and beliefs is that it can provide a sense of clarity and direction in your life. When you have a clear understanding of what matters most to you, it becomes easier to make decisions and take action that aligns with your goals and aspirations. This can help to reduce feelings of confusion, uncertainty, and overwhelm, and provide a sense of purpose and meaning in your daily life.

Another benefit is that identifying your core values and beliefs can help to build resilience and mental strength. When you have a strong sense of what matters most to you, it becomes easier to navigate the ups and downs of life with grace and determination. By focusing on your values and beliefs during times of challenge or adversity, you can find the strength to persevere and overcome obstacles.

Additionally, identifying your core values and beliefs can help to improve your overall well-being and satisfaction with life. Studies have shown that individuals who live in alignment with their values and beliefs report higher levels of happiness, fulfillment, and life satisfaction. By making choices and taking action that aligns with what matters most to you, you can create a sense of inner peace and contentment in your life.

It's also worth noting that identifying your core values and beliefs can have a positive impact on your relationships with others. When you have a clear understanding of what matters most to you, it becomes easier to communicate your needs and boundaries with others. By living in alignment with your values and beliefs, you can attract like-minded individuals into your life and build stronger, more meaningful connections with others.

In conclusion, identifying your core values and beliefs is a powerful tool for creating a fulfilling and successful life. By providing clarity and direction, building resilience and mental strength, improving well-being and satisfaction, and enhancing relationships with others, this process can have a profound impact on every aspect of your life. So take the time to reflect on your values and beliefs, and use this knowledge to guide your path towards a more meaningful and fulfilling life.

Chapter 3
Why asking "why" is essential for success

S uccess means different things to different people. For some, it might be achieving financial freedom, while for others, it could be personal fulfillment or making a positive impact on the world. Regardless of what success means to you, one thing is clear: the road to success is never easy. It requires hard work, perseverance, and a clear sense of purpose.

In this chapter, we will explore why asking "why" is essential for success. We will discuss the power of curiosity and questioning assumptions, the benefits of self-discovery and personal growth, and the structure of the book.

3.1 The power of curiosity and questioning assumptions

Asking "why" is at the heart of curiosity. Curiosity is a fundamental human trait that drives us to seek new knowledge and experiences. It's what leads us to explore the world around us and discover new things. Without curiosity, we would never have made the progress we have today in science, technology, and other fields.

However, curiosity is not just about asking questions. It's also about questioning assumptions. Assumptions are beliefs that we take for granted as true without questioning them. They can be limiting and prevent us from seeing things in new ways. By questioning assumptions, we can challenge our beliefs and open ourselves up to new possibilities.

Asking "why" can also help us to stay motivated and focused on our goals. When we have a clear sense of purpose and understand why we are working towards our goals, we are more likely to stay committed and put in the effort required to achieve them. Without a clear "why," it's easy to get discouraged and give up when we encounter obstacles or setbacks.

Moreover, asking "why" can also help us to think critically and make better decisions. By questioning assumptions and seeking out information, we can make more informed choices that are based on evidence and reason, rather than simply following what others have done or what we assume to be true. This can be particularly important when making big decisions that can have a significant impact on our lives or the lives of others.

Another benefit of asking "why" is that it can lead to innovation and creativity. By questioning the status quo and seeking out new perspectives and ideas, we can generate innovative solutions to problems and come up with creative new ways of doing things. This is particularly important in today's rapidly changing world, where new challenges and opportunities are constantly emerging.

Asking "why" is an essential tool for success in all aspects of life. It can help us to be more curious, self-aware, motivated, and focused, as well as to make better decisions and generate new ideas. In the following chapters, we will explore in more detail how asking "why" can help us to define our purpose, overcome obstacles, cultivate a growth mindset, build effective habits and routines, develop strong relationships and networks, stay adaptable and continuously learn, and prioritize our well-being.

When we approach life with a sense of curiosity and a willingness to question assumptions, we open ourselves up to new possibilities and opportunities. Curiosity allows us to explore the world around us, to learn new things, and to grow as individuals.

Questioning assumptions, on the other hand, allows us to challenge conventional wisdom and to break free from limiting beliefs and patterns of thought. By questioning assumptions, we can see things from different perspectives and gain a deeper understanding of ourselves and the world around us.

Furthermore, curiosity and questioning assumptions are essential for innovation and creativity. When we are curious about how things work and why they are the way they are, we are more likely to discover new ideas and solutions to problems. By questioning assumptions and exploring new possibilities, we can generate innovative solutions and come up with creative new ways of doing things.

Moreover, curiosity and questioning assumptions are key ingredients for effective communication and collaboration. When we approach conversations and interactions with curiosity, we are more likely to listen attentively and to ask thoughtful questions that deepen our understanding of others. By questioning assumptions and seeking out diverse perspectives, we can build stronger relationships and create more effective teams.

Curiosity and questioning assumptions are essential for personal growth and development. When we are curious about ourselves and our experiences, we are more likely to reflect on our thoughts, feelings, and behaviors, and to identify areas where we can grow and improve. By questioning our assumptions about ourselves and the world around us, we can break free from limiting beliefs and behaviors, and develop new skills and habits that help us to achieve our goals.

The power of curiosity and questioning assumptions is also important for decision-making. When we approach a decision with curiosity, we are more likely to gather information and weigh different options. By questioning assumptions about what we think we know, we can challenge our biases and make more informed and objective decisions.

Moreover, curiosity and questioning assumptions can help us to embrace uncertainty and change. When we are curious about the unknown and willing to question assumptions about what is possible, we are better equipped to adapt to new situations and to navigate uncertainty. This can help us to be more flexible and resilient in the face of change, and to take advantage of new opportunities as they arise.

Curiosity and questioning assumptions can lead to a deeper sense of meaning and purpose. When we are curious about the world around us and willing to question our assumptions about what is important, we can discover our passions and values. This can help us to live a more fulfilling life, and to pursue goals that are meaningful to us.

Furthermore, curiosity and questioning assumptions can foster empathy and understanding. When we approach others with curiosity and a willingness to question our assumptions about them, we can better understand their perspectives and experiences. This can help us to build stronger relationships, to communicate more effectively, and to work collaboratively towards common goals.

Finally, the power of curiosity and questioning assumptions can lead to a greater sense of wonder and awe. When we approach the world with a sense of curiosity and openness, we are more likely to be amazed by the beauty and complexity of the world around us. This can inspire us to live more fully and to appreciate the world in all its richness.

The power of curiosity and questioning assumptions is a fundamental aspect of human nature that has been essential for our survival and progress throughout history. Curiosity has driven our desire to explore and discover new things, to understand the world around us, and to create innovative solutions to the challenges we face. Questioning assumptions has allowed us to challenge the status quo, to see beyond the limitations of our current understanding, and to create new possibilities for the future.

In today's rapidly changing world, the power of curiosity and questioning assumptions is more important than ever. With the pace of technological innovation and the complexities of modern society, we are constantly faced with new challenges and opportunities that require us to think critically and creatively. By embracing curiosity and questioning assumptions, we can cultivate the skills and mindset needed to navigate these challenges and to create a better future for ourselves and others.

One key benefit of curiosity and questioning assumptions is that it helps us to stay open-minded and adaptable. In a world that is constantly changing, it is essential to remain flexible and to be willing to adapt to new circumstances. By staying curious and questioning our assumptions, we can avoid becoming rigid in our thinking and approach new situations with a sense of curiosity and openness. This allows us to learn and grow from our experiences and to develop new insights and perspectives.

Another important benefit of curiosity and questioning assumptions is that it helps us to develop empathy and understanding for others. By questioning our assumptions about people and their motivations, we can gain a deeper understanding of their perspectives and experiences. This can help us to build stronger relationships and to communicate more effectively, both in our personal and professional lives.

Moreover, curiosity and questioning assumptions can help us to foster a sense of wonder and awe about the world around us. By approaching the world with a sense of curiosity and openness, we are more likely to be inspired by the beauty and complexity of the natural world, the richness of human culture, and the endless possibilities for discovery and innovation. This can help us to find joy and meaning in our lives and to appreciate the world in all its diversity and complexity.

3.2 The benefits of self-discovery and personal growth

Self-discovery and personal growth are essential for living a fulfilling and meaningful life. Through the process of self-discovery, we gain a deeper understanding of ourselves and our place in the world, while personal growth helps us to develop the skills, knowledge, and mindset needed to achieve our goals and aspirations.

One of the key benefits of self-discovery and personal growth is increased self-awareness. By exploring our thoughts, feelings, and behaviors, we can gain a better understanding of our strengths and weaknesses, as well as our values and beliefs. This self-awareness can help us to make better decisions, communicate more effectively, and build stronger relationships with others.

Another benefit of self-discovery and personal growth is increased resilience. When we are aware of our strengths and weaknesses, we are better equipped to navigate challenges and setbacks. Through personal growth, we can develop skills such as problem-solving, emotional regulation, and adaptability, which enable us to bounce back from adversity and persevere in the face of challenges.

In addition, self-discovery and personal growth can lead to greater authenticity and alignment with our values and goals. By exploring our identity and purpose, we can gain a clearer sense of what matters most to us and what we want to achieve in life. This clarity can help us to make choices that are in line with our values and aspirations, and to live a more authentic and fulfilling life.

Moreover, self-discovery and personal growth can lead to increased creativity and innovation. By exploring new perspectives and ideas, we can expand our thinking and generate new solutions to problems. Personal growth can also help us to develop skills such as critical thinking, collaboration, and communication, which are essential for innovation and creativity.

Self-discovery and personal growth can improve our overall well-being. When we are aligned with our values and goals, and have the skills and mindset needed to navigate challenges, we are more likely to experience positive emotions such as joy, contentment, and fulfillment. Personal growth can also help us to develop healthy habits such as mindfulness, self-care, and exercise, which can improve our physical and mental health.

Self-discovery and personal growth can also lead to greater confidence and self-esteem. When we have a better understanding of ourselves, our strengths, and our values, we are more confident in our abilities and our decision-making. Personal growth can also help us to develop skills such as assertiveness, self-advocacy, and goal-setting, which can further boost our confidence and self-esteem.

Moreover, self-discovery and personal growth can enhance our relationships with others. By developing self-awareness and emotional intelligence, we can better understand and empathize with others. This can lead to improved communication, greater trust, and deeper connections with others. Personal growth can also help us to develop skills such as active listening, conflict resolution, and boundary-setting, which are essential for healthy relationships.

In addition, self-discovery and personal growth can lead to greater purpose and meaning in life. By exploring our values and goals, we can develop a clearer sense of our purpose and what we want to achieve in life. This sense of purpose can provide a sense of direction and motivation, and can help us to live a more fulfilling and meaningful life.

Self-discovery and personal growth can help us to overcome limiting beliefs and negative self-talk. By exploring our thoughts and beliefs, we can identify patterns of thinking that may be holding us back, and develop strategies to challenge and reframe them. Personal growth can also help us to develop a more positive and compassionate mindset, which can improve our mental health and well-being.

Self-discovery and personal growth can help us to cultivate a growth mindset. By embracing a mindset of learning and growth, we can approach challenges and setbacks as opportunities for learning and development. This can help us to overcome fear of failure, take risks, and pursue our goals with greater confidence and resilience.

Self-discovery and personal growth can lead to a greater sense of fulfillment and happiness. When we are aligned with our values and purpose, and are growing and learning, we are more likely to experience positive emotions such as joy, contentment, and gratitude. Personal growth can also help us to develop healthy coping strategies for stress and adversity, which can improve our overall well-being.

Self-discovery and personal growth can also improve our physical health. Research has shown that chronic stress, anxiety, and negative emotions can have a negative impact on our physical health, increasing our risk for various health problems such as heart disease, diabetes, and obesity. By developing healthy coping strategies and improving our mental health and well-being through personal growth, we can reduce our risk for these health problems.

In addition, self-discovery and personal growth can lead to greater creativity and innovation. When we are open to exploring new ideas and perspectives, we are more likely to come up with creative solutions to problems and to develop innovative ideas. Personal growth can also help us to develop a growth mindset, which encourages us to take risks and embrace failure as an opportunity for learning and growth, leading to more innovative thinking.

Self-discovery and personal growth can improve our career prospects and success. By developing skills such as self-awareness, emotional intelligence, and communication, we can become more effective leaders, collaborators, and problem-solvers in the workplace. Personal growth can also help us to identify our strengths and passions, and to pursue careers and opportunities that are aligned with our values and purpose.

Moreover, self-discovery and personal growth can improve our financial well-being. By developing financial literacy and habits, we can become better at managing our finances and building wealth. Personal growth can also help us to identify our financial goals and values, and to make financial decisions that are aligned with our long-term aspirations.

Self-discovery and personal growth can improve our sense of community and social responsibility. By developing a greater understanding of ourselves and others, and by cultivating a sense of empathy and compassion, we are more likely to become active and engaged members of our communities. Personal growth can also help us to identify issues and causes that we are passionate about, and to become advocates for social justice and positive change.

They can lead to a greater sense of spiritual connection and fulfillment. By exploring our spirituality and connection to something greater than ourselves, we can develop a greater sense of purpose and meaning in life. Personal growth can also help us to cultivate practices such as mindfulness, meditation, and gratitude, which can deepen our spiritual connection and improve our overall well-being.

One of the most significant benefits of self-discovery and personal growth is increased self-confidence. When we have a better understanding of our strengths and weaknesses, values, and passions, we are more confident in our abilities and decisions. This self-assurance can help us to overcome challenges and take on new opportunities with greater ease, leading to greater success and fulfillment.

Personal growth can also lead to improved relationships. When we are more self-aware and emotionally intelligent, we are better able to communicate and connect with others. We are more empathetic and understanding, which can improve our relationships with family, friends, coworkers, and romantic partners. Additionally, personal growth can help us to establish healthier boundaries and more fulfilling relationships, leading to greater happiness and well-being.

Moreover, self-discovery and personal growth can help us to develop a greater sense of resilience and adaptability. Life is full of challenges and setbacks, but by cultivating resilience and adaptability, we can bounce back from difficulties more quickly and effectively. Personal growth can help us to develop coping strategies, such as mindfulness, gratitude, and positive self-talk, which can improve our ability to navigate adversity.

Another benefit of self-discovery and personal growth is improved decision-making. By developing greater self-awareness and emotional intelligence, we are better equipped to make decisions that are aligned with our values, goals, and purpose. We are less likely to be swayed by external pressures or influenced by our biases and assumptions, leading to more intentional and fulfilling decisions.

They can lead to greater satisfaction and happiness in life. When we are living in alignment with our values and purpose, and pursuing opportunities that bring us joy and fulfillment, we are more likely to experience a sense of contentment and happiness. Personal growth can help us to identify the things that truly matter to us, and to pursue a life that is rich in meaning and purpose.

Furthermore, self-discovery and personal growth can help us to break free from limiting beliefs and self-doubt. Many of us have internalized negative beliefs or self-doubt that hold us back from pursuing our dreams or taking risks. Through self-discovery and personal growth, we can challenge these beliefs and develop a more positive and empowering mindset, leading to greater success and happiness.

Self-discovery and personal growth is the ability to develop a growth mindset. A growth mindset is the belief that our abilities and intelligence can be developed through hard work and dedication, rather than being fixed traits that we are born with. When we embrace a growth mindset, we are more likely to take on challenges and pursue opportunities for learning and growth, rather than being held back by fear of failure or limiting beliefs.

Self-discovery and personal growth can help us to develop greater self-compassion and kindness towards ourselves. Many of us are our own harshest critics, and struggle with feelings of self-doubt and inadequacy. Through self-discovery and personal growth, we can learn to be more gentle and understanding towards ourselves, and to cultivate greater self-love and acceptance.

Personal growth can also lead to greater creativity and innovation. When we are living in alignment with our values and purpose, and pursuing opportunities that bring us joy and fulfillment, we are more likely to be inspired and creative. Personal growth can help us to tap into our natural creativity and innovation, leading to greater success and impact in our personal and professional lives.

Self-discovery and personal growth can help us to develop a greater sense of meaning and purpose in life. When we are living in alignment with our values and purpose, we are more likely to feel a sense of connection to something greater than ourselves, and to feel that our lives have meaning and significance. Personal growth can help us to identify our purpose and passions, and to pursue a life that is aligned with our deepest desires and aspirations.

Additionally, self-discovery and personal growth can lead to greater financial success and abundance. When we are living in alignment with our values and purpose, we are more likely to pursue opportunities that are financially rewarding and fulfilling. Personal growth can help us to develop the skills and mindset necessary for financial success, such as financial literacy, goal-setting, and risk-taking.

Chapter 4
The Importance of Defining Your "Why"

Defining your "why" is crucial for achieving success and fulfillment in life. When you have a clear understanding of why you are pursuing a particular goal or dream, you are more likely to stay motivated and committed, even when faced with obstacles or setbacks.

Without a clear sense of purpose or direction, it's easy to get lost in the day-to-day tasks and lose sight of the bigger picture. Defining your "why" helps to provide clarity and focus, allowing you to prioritize the actions that will lead you to your goals.

Having a defined "why" can help you to make more intentional and fulfilling decisions. When you know why you are pursuing a particular path or opportunity, you are better able to evaluate whether it aligns with your values, passions, and purpose. This can help you to avoid wasting time and energy on pursuits that don't bring you fulfillment or happiness.

Defining your "why" can help you to overcome obstacles and challenges. When faced with difficulties, it's easy to become discouraged and lose motivation. However, when you have a clear sense of purpose and passion, you are more likely to push through these challenges and keep moving forward.

In addition, defining your "why" can help you to communicate your goals and vision to others. When you are able to articulate your purpose and vision clearly, you can inspire and motivate others to support and join you in your journey.

Furthermore, defining your "why" can help you to build a strong personal brand or business identity. When you have a clear sense of purpose and values, you can build a brand that is authentic and aligned with your vision. This can help you to attract clients or customers who share your values and vision, leading to greater success and impact.

Another benefit of defining your "why" is that it helps you to stay true to yourself and your values. When you have a clear sense of your purpose and passions, you are less likely to be swayed by external influences or the opinions of others. This can help you to make decisions that are true to your authentic self, leading to greater satisfaction and fulfillment.

Defining your "why" can help you to set meaningful and achievable goals. When you have a clear sense of purpose, you are better able to identify goals that align with your values and contribute to your overall vision. This can help you to avoid setting goals that are superficial or unfulfilling, leading to greater motivation and progress.

Defining your "why" can help you to develop a growth mindset. When you approach your goals with a growth mindset, you are open to learning and feedback, and you see obstacles as opportunities for growth and development. This can help you to achieve greater success and reach your full potential.

Defining your "why" can help you to cultivate a sense of gratitude and appreciation for the present moment. When you have a clear sense of purpose and passion, you are more likely to appreciate the journey and the small wins along the way. This can help you to develop a positive mindset and increase your overall sense of well-being.

It can help you to become a more effective leader. When you have a clear sense of your values and vision, you can inspire and motivate others to follow you in pursuit of a common goal. This can help you to build a strong and cohesive team, leading to greater success and impact.

Another benefit of defining your "why" is that it can help you to overcome challenges and adversity. When you have a clear sense of your purpose and passion, you are more likely to persevere through difficult times and setbacks. This can help you to develop resilience and grit, which are essential qualities for achieving success.

It helps you to create a sense of alignment in your life. When your actions and goals are in alignment with your purpose and values, you are more likely to feel a sense of flow and ease in your life. This can help you to reduce stress and anxiety and increase your overall sense of well-being.

Defining your "why" can help you to build a strong personal brand. When you have a clear sense of your values and vision, you can create a consistent and authentic personal brand that reflects who you are and what you stand for. This can help you to attract opportunities and build a reputation as a trusted and respected leader in your field.

Furthermore, defining your "why" can help you to create a legacy that you can be proud of. When you have a clear sense of purpose and passion, you can identify ways to make a meaningful and lasting impact on the world around you. This can help you to leave a positive mark on the world and create a sense of purpose that extends beyond your own lifetime. Finally, It can help you to live a more intentional and fulfilling life. When you have a clear sense of purpose and passion, you are more likely to make choices that align with your values and contribute to your overall vision. This can help you to live a life that is true to your authentic self and brings you joy and fulfillment.

4.1 Why having a clear purpose and vision is crucial for success

Having a clear purpose and vision is crucial for success because it provides direction and focus. When you have a clear sense of purpose and vision, you know what you want to achieve and where you want to go. This clarity can help you to make decisions that are aligned with your goals and values, which can lead to more successful outcomes.

Having a clear purpose and vision can help you to stay motivated and committed to your goals. When you have a sense of purpose and a vision for your life, you are more likely to stay focused on your goals, even when faced with challenges and obstacles. This can help you to overcome setbacks and stay on track towards achieving your desired outcomes.

A clear purpose and vision can help you to prioritize your time and resources. When you have a sense of what is important to you and what you want to achieve, you can focus on activities and projects that are aligned with your goals and values. This can help you to use your time and resources more effectively and efficiently, which can lead to greater success.

A clear purpose and vision can help you to create a sense of meaning and fulfillment in your life. When you have a sense of purpose and a vision for your life, you are more likely to feel fulfilled and satisfied with your life's direction. This can help you to live a more meaningful and purposeful life, which can contribute to greater happiness and well-being.

Having a clear purpose and vision can also help you to identify and pursue opportunities that are aligned with your goals and values. When you have a sense of what you want to achieve, you are more likely to recognize opportunities that can help you to move towards your desired outcomes. This can lead to greater success and fulfillment in both your personal and professional life.

Having a clear purpose and vision can help you to communicate your goals and values more effectively to others. When you are able to articulate your purpose and vision clearly, you can inspire and motivate others to support your goals and vision. This can help you to build strong relationships and networks that can contribute to your success.

Furthermore, having a clear purpose and vision can help you to stay resilient in the face of challenges and setbacks. When you have a clear sense of what you want to achieve, you are more likely to persist in the face of obstacles and adversity. This can help you to develop resilience and grit, which are essential qualities for success.

Additionally, having a clear purpose and vision can help you to stay focused on the big picture. When you have a sense of what you want to achieve, you can avoid getting bogged down in details and distractions that can detract from your progress. This can help you to stay focused on your long-term goals and to avoid getting sidetracked by short-term setbacks.

Therefore, having a clear purpose and vision is crucial for success because it provides direction, focus, motivation, and meaning. By taking the time to define your purpose and vision, you can unlock your full potential and create a life that is truly fulfilling and purposeful.

4.2 How to identify and clarify your values and goals

Identifying and clarifying your values and goals is an important step in defining your "why" and achieving success. To identify your values, you can start by reflecting on what is most important to you and what gives your life meaning and purpose. Ask yourself questions such as: What do I stand for? What kind of person do I want to be? What kind of impact do I want to have on the world? Once you have identified your values, you can prioritize them based on their importance to you.

To clarify your goals, start by setting specific, measurable, achievable, relevant, and time-bound (SMART) goals. Think about what you want to achieve in different areas of your life, such as career, relationships, health, and personal development. Write down your goals and break them down into smaller, actionable steps that you can take to achieve them.

It is also important to review and revise your values and goals regularly. As you grow and evolve, your values and goals may change, and it is important to ensure that they are still aligned with your current priorities and aspirations.

To clarify your values and goals is to seek feedback and support from others. Talk to people who know you well, such as friends, family, or mentors, and ask for their input on your values and goals. They may be able to provide valuable insights and feedback that can help you to refine and clarify your "why."

Consider seeking guidance from a coach or counselor who can help you to explore and clarify your values and goals in greater depth. They can provide tools and techniques that can help you to gain greater clarity and focus, as well as overcome any barriers or obstacles that may be preventing you from achieving your goals.

Identifying and clarifying your values and goals is an essential step in defining your "why" and achieving success. By reflecting on what is most important to you, setting SMART goals, reviewing and revising your values and goals regularly, seeking feedback and support from others, and seeking guidance from a coach or counselor, you can unlock your full potential and create a life that is truly fulfilling and purposeful.

Another way to identify and clarify your values and goals is through self-reflection and journaling. Writing down your thoughts and feelings can help you to gain greater clarity and understanding of what is important to you and what you want to achieve in your life. You can use prompts such as "What are my strengths and weaknesses?" or "What are my passions and interests?" to guide your reflection.

In addition, it is important to ensure that your values and goals are aligned with each other. Your goals should reflect your values and help you to live in accordance with them. For example, if one of your values is family, your goals may include spending more time with your loved ones or finding a job that allows you to balance work and family life.

It is also important to consider the potential obstacles and challenges that may arise as you work towards your goals. By anticipating these challenges and developing a plan to overcome them, you can increase your chances of success. For example, if your goal is to start your own business, you may need to overcome financial challenges or learn new skills. Developing a plan to address these challenges can help you to stay motivated and focused.

Another helpful tool for identifying and clarifying your values and goals is visualization. Visualizing yourself achieving your goals and living in accordance with your values can help to increase your motivation and commitment. You can create a vision board or visualize yourself achieving your goals in your mind's eye.

Therefore, it is important to remember that identifying and clarifying your values and goals is an ongoing process. As you grow and evolve, your values and goals may change, and it is important to be open to this change and adapt your goals accordingly. By staying flexible and open-minded, you can continue to refine and clarify your "why" and achieve greater success and fulfillment in your life.

4.3 The role of motivation and inspiration in achieving your "why"

Motivation and inspiration play a critical role in achieving your "why". While identifying your purpose and setting clear goals are important, it is your motivation and inspiration that will help you stay on track, persevere through challenges, and continue moving towards your desired outcome.

Motivation is the driving force behind your actions. It is what inspires you to take action towards your goals, even when you may not feel like it. There are two types of motivation - intrinsic and extrinsic. Intrinsic motivation comes from within, and is driven by your personal values, beliefs, and goals. Extrinsic motivation, on the other hand, comes from external factors such as rewards, recognition, and social pressure.

Intrinsic motivation is often more powerful than extrinsic motivation, as it is rooted in your personal values and goals. When you are intrinsically motivated, you are more likely to stay committed to your goals and persist through challenges. To cultivate intrinsic motivation, it is important to align your goals with your personal values, and to find meaning and purpose in the work you do.

Inspiration, on the other hand, comes from external sources such as people, events, and experiences. Inspiration can come from a variety of sources, such as successful entrepreneurs, athletes, artists, or family members. When you are inspired, you are more likely to be creative, persistent, and resilient in pursuing your goals.

To cultivate inspiration, it is important to seek out people and experiences that align with your values and goals. This may involve attending seminars or workshops, reading books or articles, or networking with like-minded individuals. By surrounding yourself with sources of inspiration, you can stay motivated and energized in pursuing your goals.

In addition to motivation and inspiration, it is also important to stay focused and disciplined in pursuing your goals. This may involve creating a plan of action, setting clear and specific goals, and holding yourself accountable for your progress. It may also involve seeking support and guidance from mentors, coaches, or friends.

One way to stay motivated and inspired is to surround yourself with positive and supportive people. These individuals can provide encouragement, guidance, and accountability as you pursue your goals. Seek out mentors, coaches, or friends who share similar values and goals, and who can offer insights and advice based on their own experiences.

Another important factor in staying motivated and inspired is to maintain a growth mindset. This involves embracing challenges and setbacks as opportunities for learning and growth, rather than seeing them as roadblocks to success. By adopting a growth mindset, you can stay resilient and persistent in pursuing your goals, even when faced with obstacles or setbacks.

Visualization can also be a powerful tool for staying motivated and inspired. This involves creating a mental image of your desired outcome, and focusing on that image as you work towards your goals. By visualizing your success, you can stay motivated and focused, and increase your chances of achieving your desired outcome.

Setting realistic and achievable goals is also important for staying motivated and inspired. Break your goals down into smaller, manageable steps, and track your progress along the way. Celebrate your successes, no matter how small, and use them as fuel to keep moving forward.

It is important to stay true to yourself and your values as you pursue your goals. Remember that success is not just about achieving external milestones or accomplishments, but also about living a life that aligns with your personal values and beliefs. By staying true to yourself and your vision, you can achieve greater success and fulfillment in all areas of your life.

Another important aspect of maintaining motivation and inspiration is to regularly reflect on your progress and adjust your approach as needed. This involves being honest with yourself about what is working and what is not, and being willing to make changes when necessary. Use feedback from others, as well as your own self-reflection, to identify areas where you can improve, and make a plan to address these areas.

It is also important to celebrate your successes along the way. Acknowledge the progress you have made and the hard work you have put in, and take time to appreciate your accomplishments. Celebrating your successes can help you maintain a positive attitude and momentum as you continue working towards your goals.

Surrounding yourself with like-minded individuals can also be a powerful source of motivation and inspiration. Seek out communities or groups that share your interests and values, and engage with them regularly. This can help you stay accountable, share ideas and resources, and gain new insights and perspectives.

Maintaining motivation and inspiration is a crucial part of achieving your "why". By regularly reflecting on your progress, celebrating your successes, surrounding yourself with like-minded individuals, and embracing setbacks as opportunities for growth, you can stay motivated and inspired as you work towards your goals.

Finally, it is important to remember that setbacks and failures are a natural part of the journey towards achieving your "why". Rather than letting these setbacks discourage you, use them as an opportunity to learn and grow. Ask yourself what you can learn from the experience, and how you can use this knowledge to move forward in a more effective way.

Chapter 5
Developing a Growth Mindset

Overcoming self-doubt and fear is a crucial step on the road to achieving success. Self-doubt and fear can prevent us from taking risks, pursuing our goals, and realizing our full potential. However, with the right mindset and tools, it is possible to overcome these obstacles and move forward with confidence.

One key strategy for overcoming self-doubt and fear is to reframe negative thoughts and beliefs. Instead of focusing on what could go wrong or why you might fail, try to focus on the potential for growth and learning. Consider reframing your self-talk to focus on your strengths and accomplishments, and remind yourself of times when you have successfully overcome challenges in the past.

Another strategy is to practice self-compassion. Self-compassion involves treating yourself with the same kindness and understanding that you would offer to a friend. This means being gentle with yourself when you make mistakes, and recognizing that failure is a natural part of the learning process. By practicing self-compassion, you can reduce feelings of self-doubt and fear, and increase your confidence and resilience.

It can also be helpful to set realistic goals and take small, manageable steps towards achieving them. By breaking down larger goals into smaller, more achievable tasks, you can reduce feelings of overwhelm and increase your sense of accomplishment. This can help build momentum and confidence as you work towards your larger goals.

In addition, seeking support from others can be an effective way to overcome self-doubt and fear. This might involve seeking feedback and guidance from a mentor or coach, or simply connecting with friends and family who offer encouragement and support. Being part of a supportive community can help you stay motivated, maintain perspective, and build confidence in your abilities.

Overcoming self-doubt and fear is an important part of achieving success. By reframing negative thoughts, practicing self-compassion, setting realistic goals, seeking support from others, and acknowledging the normalcy of these emotions, you can build the confidence and resilience you need to pursue your goals with courage and determination.

Finally, it is important to recognize that self-doubt and fear are normal, and that everyone experiences these feelings at some point. Rather than trying to eliminate these emotions entirely, focus on developing strategies to manage them and move forward in spite of them.

5.1 Why a growth mindset is essential for learning and development

A growth mindset is essential for learning and development because it allows us to approach challenges and obstacles with a positive and open mindset. Rather than viewing failure as a reflection of our abilities or potential, a growth mindset encourages us to see failure as an opportunity for learning and growth. This mindset can lead to greater resilience, motivation, and ultimately, success.

With a growth mindset, individuals believe that their abilities and potential are not fixed, but rather can be developed through hard work, perseverance, and a willingness to learn. This perspective encourages individuals to embrace challenges, take risks, and learn from their mistakes. In contrast, a fixed mindset assumes that our abilities and potential are predetermined and unchangeable, leading to a fear of failure and a lack of motivation to take on new challenges.

Research has shown that individuals with a growth mindset are more likely to succeed academically, professionally, and personally. They are more resilient in the face of setbacks, more likely to persist in the face of obstacles, and more willing to take risks to achieve their goals. A growth mindset also promotes a love of learning, as individuals are more likely to see learning as a lifelong pursuit rather than a means to an end.

To cultivate a growth mindset, it is important to focus on effort and progress rather than on outcomes. Rather than measuring success solely by the end result, individuals with a growth mindset focus on the process of learning and development. They embrace challenges and view mistakes as opportunities for growth, and they seek feedback to learn and improve.

It is also important to acknowledge that the journey of learning and development is not always easy, and setbacks and failures are inevitable. However, with a growth mindset, individuals can learn to embrace these challenges and view them as opportunities for growth and development. By adopting a growth mindset, individuals can develop the resilience, motivation, and confidence needed to achieve their goals and reach their full potential.

A growth mindset is essential for learning and development as it allows individuals to approach challenges with a positive and open mindset, embrace failure as an opportunity for learning and growth, and ultimately achieve greater success and fulfillment. By cultivating a growth mindset, individuals can develop the resilience, motivation, and confidence needed to pursue their goals and reach their full potential.

Having a growth mindset means that one believes in the ability to develop and improve their skills and abilities through dedication and hard work. This mindset allows individuals to approach new situations with a positive attitude and a willingness to learn, even if they do not have all the answers or the necessary skills at first.

With a growth mindset, individuals can also develop resilience and grit, which are important traits for achieving success. Resilience allows individuals to bounce back from setbacks and challenges, while grit gives them the determination to persist in the face of obstacles.

Moreover, a growth mindset encourages individuals to seek out feedback and constructive criticism as a means to improve and grow. It also helps individuals to develop a sense of curiosity and a desire to learn, which can lead to personal and professional growth.

In contrast, individuals with a fixed mindset believe that their abilities are innate and unchangeable. They may view challenges and setbacks as evidence of their limitations rather than opportunities for growth. This can lead to a fear of failure and a lack of motivation to try new things or take on challenges.

In addition to promoting resilience and a desire to learn, a growth mindset can also lead to increased creativity and innovation. When individuals believe that their abilities can be developed through effort and hard work, they are more likely to take risks and think outside the box.

Moreover, a growth mindset can help individuals to develop a sense of purpose and meaning in their lives. When individuals are motivated by the belief that they can improve and develop their skills, they are more likely to pursue goals that align with their values and passions.

On the other hand, individuals with a fixed mindset may be more likely to avoid challenges or shy away from pursuing their goals because they believe that their abilities are fixed and limited.

Fortunately, a growth mindset can be cultivated through deliberate effort and practice. By focusing on the process of learning and development, rather than just the end result, individuals can begin to adopt a growth mindset and reap the many benefits it offers.

Some ways to cultivate a growth mindset include seeking out challenging experiences, embracing mistakes and failures as opportunities to learn, and focusing on the process of learning rather than just the outcome. It can also be helpful to surround oneself with supportive and encouraging people who share a growth mindset.

Another benefit of having a growth mindset is that it can lead to a greater sense of self-awareness and self-reflection. When individuals believe that their abilities can be developed through effort and hard work, they are more likely to take responsibility for their own growth and development.

This can lead to a greater understanding of one's strengths and weaknesses, as well as a willingness to seek out feedback and constructive criticism in order to improve. In turn, this can lead to greater self-confidence and a stronger sense of self-efficacy.

Furthermore, having a growth mindset can help individuals to overcome obstacles and setbacks more effectively. Rather than viewing challenges and setbacks as evidence of their limitations or lack of ability, individuals with a growth mindset see them as opportunities to learn and grow. They are more likely to persist in the face of adversity and to view mistakes and failures as a natural part of the learning process. This can lead to greater resilience and perseverance, as well as a more positive attitude towards challenges and setbacks.

In addition to the benefits already mentioned, having a growth mindset can also lead to more creativity and innovation. When individuals believe that their abilities can be developed, they are more likely to experiment with new ideas and approaches, and to take risks in order to achieve their goals.

This can lead to the development of new and innovative solutions to problems, as well as the creation of new products, services, and businesses. In turn, this can lead to greater success and fulfillment in both personal and professional endeavors.

Another benefit of having a growth mindset is that it can lead to better relationships and communication skills. When individuals are open to learning and growth, they are more likely to listen to others, seek out different perspectives, and communicate effectively.

This can lead to more positive and fulfilling relationships with family, friends, and colleagues, as well as greater success in the workplace. Furthermore, individuals with a growth mindset are more likely to be effective leaders, as they are able to inspire and motivate others to achieve their goals and reach their full potential.

Finally, having a growth mindset can lead to greater happiness and well-being. When individuals believe that their abilities can be developed, they are less likely to experience feelings of helplessness and hopelessness, and more likely to feel empowered and in control of their lives.

This can lead to greater overall life satisfaction, as well as improved physical and mental health. Studies have shown that individuals with a growth mindset are less likely to suffer from anxiety and depression, and more likely to experience positive emotions such as happiness, joy, and fulfillment.

In summary, having a growth mindset is essential for personal and professional growth and success. It can lead to greater self-awareness, resilience, and self-efficacy, as well as more creativity, innovation, and effective communication skills. It can also lead to greater happiness and well-being, and ultimately, a more fulfilling and successful life.

5.2 How to cultivate a growth mindset through mindset shifts and habits

Developing a growth mindset can take time and effort, but it is a valuable tool for achieving personal and professional success. Fortunately, there are several strategies that can help individuals cultivate a growth mindset and shift away from a fixed mindset.

One important mindset shift is to view challenges as opportunities for growth and learning, rather than as obstacles to be avoided or feared. By embracing challenges and viewing them as chances to develop new skills and abilities, individuals can begin to approach new tasks with greater confidence and enthusiasm.

Another key strategy is to reframe failures and setbacks as learning experiences. Instead of viewing mistakes as signs of personal inadequacy or incompetence, individuals with a growth mindset see them as opportunities to learn and improve. This can involve reflecting on what went wrong, identifying areas for improvement, and developing new strategies for success.

Additionally, individuals can cultivate a growth mindset by seeking out new experiences and challenges. By embracing new opportunities and stepping outside of their comfort zones, individuals can expand their skills and knowledge, and develop a sense of resilience and adaptability.

Cultivating a growth mindset can also involve developing positive habits and routines that support learning and growth. This can include setting goals, practicing self-reflection, seeking feedback and constructive criticism, and prioritizing continuous learning and development.

Overall, developing a growth mindset is a valuable tool for achieving personal and professional success. By embracing challenges, reframing failures, seeking out new experiences, and developing positive habits and routines, individuals can cultivate a mindset that supports ongoing learning and development, and empowers them to achieve their full potential.

In addition to the strategies outlined above, there are several other ways that individuals can cultivate a growth mindset and shift away from a fixed mindset.

One key strategy is to develop a sense of curiosity and a love of learning. This can involve seeking out new information and perspectives, asking questions, and actively seeking to expand one's knowledge and understanding of the world. By viewing learning as an ongoing process, rather than a finite goal, individuals can cultivate a mindset of continuous improvement and growth.

Another important aspect of cultivating a growth mindset is to practice self-compassion and positive self-talk. This can involve reframing negative self-talk and self-criticism, and instead focusing on one's strengths, accomplishments, and potential. By developing a more positive and compassionate view of oneself, individuals can increase their resilience and motivation, and overcome setbacks and challenges more effectively.

Mindfulness and meditation practices can also be helpful for cultivating a growth mindset. By focusing on the present moment and practicing non-judgmental awareness of one's thoughts and emotions, individuals can develop a greater sense of inner calm and resilience. This can help individuals to stay focused on their goals, even in the face of adversity, and to approach challenges with greater clarity and perspective.

Cultivating a growth mindset can also involve developing positive relationships and seeking out mentors and role models who embody the qualities and values that one aspires to. By surrounding oneself with supportive and inspiring individuals, individuals can tap into a network of support and encouragement, and gain valuable insights and perspectives on how to achieve their goals.

Cultivating a growth mindset requires ongoing effort and commitment, but it is a valuable tool for achieving personal and professional success. By developing a sense of curiosity and love of learning, practicing self-compassion and positive self-talk, engaging in mindfulness and meditation practices, and cultivating positive relationships, individuals can shift their mindset and achieve their full potential.

To cultivate a growth mindset, it is essential to develop mindset shifts and habits that reinforce it. Here are some strategies that can help:

- Embrace challenges: Challenges can help you grow and develop new skills. Instead of shying away from challenges, embrace them as opportunities to learn and improve. Approach challenges with a positive attitude and focus on the process rather than the outcome.
- Practice self-compassion: Self-compassion involves being kind and understanding toward yourself, especially when facing setbacks and failures. Instead of beating yourself up, practice self-compassion by acknowledging your efforts and progress, and reminding yourself that mistakes and failures are a natural part of the learning process.
- Celebrate small wins: Celebrating small wins along the way can help you stay motivated and build momentum. Acknowledge and celebrate your progress, no matter how small it may seem. This can help you develop a sense of accomplishment and boost your confidence.
- Cultivate a love of learning: Adopt a curious and open-minded approach to learning. Instead of focusing on grades or performance, focus on the joy of learning and the process of acquiring new knowledge and skills. This can help you develop a lifelong love of learning and a growth mindset.
- Practice positive self-talk: The way you talk to yourself can have a big impact on your mindset. Practice positive self-talk by using encouraging and empowering language, even when facing challenges or setbacks. Instead of saying, "I can't do this," try saying, "I'm still learning and growing, and I'll keep trying."
- Emphasize effort over talent: Instead of focusing on innate talent or abilities, emphasize the importance of effort and hard work. Recognize that success is often the result of consistent effort and a willingness to persevere through challenges and setbacks.

- Surround yourself with growth-minded people: The people you surround yourself with can have a big impact on your mindset. Seek out and surround yourself with people who have a growth mindset and who inspire and encourage you to learn, grow, and develop.

A growth mindset is the belief that one's abilities and qualities can be developed through dedication and hard work. This mindset is essential for learning and development, as it encourages individuals to embrace challenges, persist through obstacles, and learn from failures.

To cultivate a growth mindset, individuals can engage in mindset shifts and develop new habits. One mindset shift is to view challenges as opportunities for growth, rather than as threats to one's abilities. When faced with a challenge, individuals with a growth mindset see it as a chance to learn and improve, rather than as a sign of incompetence.

Another mindset shift is to embrace the power of "not yet." Rather than viewing a lack of immediate success as a failure, individuals with a growth mindset see it as an opportunity to continue learning and developing. They recognize that success may not come immediately, but with continued effort and dedication, they can achieve their goals.

Developing new habits can also help cultivate a growth mindset. For example, individuals can adopt a daily practice of reflection and self-evaluation. This practice involves reflecting on one's strengths and weaknesses, identifying areas for improvement, and setting goals for growth. By regularly engaging in self-evaluation, individuals can track their progress and adjust their efforts accordingly.

Another habit to cultivate a growth mindset is to seek out new challenges and opportunities for growth. This may involve taking on new projects or roles that push one's boundaries, or seeking out feedback from others to identify areas for improvement. By embracing new challenges and seeking out feedback, individuals can continue to develop their skills and abilities.

Additionally, individuals can cultivate a growth mindset by surrounding themselves with others who have a similar mindset. This may involve seeking out mentors or colleagues who can offer guidance and support, or joining communities of like-minded individuals who share a commitment to growth and development.

Therefore, cultivating a growth mindset involves a combination of mindset shifts and new habits. By embracing challenges, persisting through obstacles, and learning from failures, individuals can develop the belief that their abilities and qualities can be developed through dedication and hard work. With a growth mindset, individuals are better equipped to learn and develop, and are more likely to achieve their goals and reach their full potential.

5.3 The connection between growth mindset and success

The connection between growth mindset and success is profound. Those who possess a growth mindset tend to approach challenges and setbacks as opportunities for learning and growth, rather than as failures or evidence of fixed abilities. This attitude allows them to persevere through challenges, embrace new challenges, and ultimately achieve greater success in their personal and professional lives.

One of the reasons why a growth mindset is so closely linked to success is that it enables individuals to develop resilience in the face of adversity. When things don't go according to plan, those with a growth mindset are less likely to give up or become discouraged. Instead, they view setbacks as opportunities to learn and improve. This approach allows them to stay motivated and continue making progress towards their goals, even when the going gets tough.

Furthermore, those with a growth mindset tend to be more open to feedback and criticism. They understand that feedback is essential for learning and improvement, and are willing to seek out and incorporate feedback in order to continue growing and developing. This openness to feedback allows them to continually improve their skills and knowledge, which in turn can lead to greater success in their personal and professional lives.

In addition to these qualities, those with a growth mindset are also more likely to take risks and try new things. They understand that failure is a natural part of the learning process, and are willing to take calculated risks in order to learn and grow. This willingness to take risks can lead to new opportunities and greater success in their chosen fields.

Ultimately, the connection between growth mindset and success is clear: those who possess a growth mindset are better equipped to handle challenges, more open to feedback and criticism, and more willing to take risks and try new things. These qualities allow them to continually learn and improve, and ultimately achieve greater success in their personal and professional lives.

The connection between growth mindset and success is well-documented in research and observed in the experiences of successful individuals across various fields. A growth mindset is the belief that intelligence and abilities can be developed through dedication and hard work. Those who possess a growth mindset view failure as an opportunity for growth and embrace challenges as a means of learning and improvement.

Individuals with a growth mindset are more likely to set challenging goals, persist in the face of obstacles, and ultimately achieve greater success than those with a fixed mindset. When faced with setbacks or failures, they are more likely to engage in self-reflection, identify areas for improvement, and develop new strategies for success.

Studies have shown that individuals with a growth mindset are more likely to exhibit resilience, perseverance, and adaptability, which are critical traits for success in today's rapidly changing world. They are better equipped to handle uncertainty and ambiguity, as they see challenges as opportunities for growth rather than insurmountable obstacles.

Moreover, individuals with a growth mindset are more likely to seek out constructive feedback and view it as a valuable tool for learning and growth. They are open to new perspectives and ideas, which allows them to continually evolve and improve their performance.

In contrast, individuals with a fixed mindset tend to view their abilities and intelligence as static and unchanging. They may avoid challenges, fearing that failure will undermine their self-image as competent and capable individuals. They may also view feedback as a threat to their self-esteem, rather than an opportunity for growth.

The connection between growth mindset and success lies in the ability to adapt and thrive in a constantly changing world. By embracing challenges, seeking out new experiences, and continuously learning and growing, individuals with a growth mindset are better equipped to achieve their goals and reach their full potential.

Individuals with a growth mindset are often more resilient in the face of setbacks and obstacles. They view challenges as opportunities for growth and learning, rather than as insurmountable barriers. This mindset allows them to persist in the face of difficulties, to embrace feedback and criticism as opportunities for improvement, and to continue developing their skills and abilities.

Individuals with a fixed mindset may be more likely to give up when faced with obstacles or setbacks, viewing them as signs of their own inadequacy or limitations. They may avoid challenges or opportunities for growth in order to protect their self-image and avoid the risk of failure.

The connection between a growth mindset and success can be seen in many different domains, from academic and professional success to personal growth and fulfillment. Individuals with a growth mindset are often more motivated, more engaged, and more persistent in pursuit of their goals. They are more likely to take on challenging projects, to seek out feedback and learning opportunities, and to continue developing their skills and abilities over time.

Overall, the benefits of cultivating a growth mindset are clear. By adopting a mindset of continuous learning and development, individuals can overcome self-doubt and fear, embrace their true potential, and achieve greater success and fulfillment in all areas of life.

© **Max Fortune**